I used to live here once

I used to live here once

The haunted life of

JEAN RHYS

Miranda Seymour

W. W. NORTON & COMPANY
Independent Publishers Since 1923

For information about permission to reproduce selections from
this book, write to Permissions, W. W. Norton & Company, Inc.
500 Fifth Avenue, New York, NY 10110

For information about special discounts for bulk purchases,
please contact W. W. Norton Special Sales at
specialsales@wwnorton.com or 800-233-4830

Manufacturing by Lake Book Manufacturing
Book design by Chris Welch
Production manager: Devon Zahn

ISBN 978-1-324-00612-1

W. W. Norton & Company, Inc.
500 Fifth Avenue, New York, N.Y. 10110
www.wwnorton.com

W. W. Norton & Company Ltd.
15 Carlisle Street, London W1D 3BS

1 2 3 4 5 6 7 8 9 0

TO LENNOX HONYCHURCH AND POLLY PATTULO,

KEEPING THE SPIRIT OF JEAN RHYS ALIVE IN DOMINICA,

THE ISLAND OF HER BIRTH; AND TO SAMANTHA MOSS,

DOING THE SAME AT RHYS'S LAST HOME IN DEVON

I would never be part of anything. I would never really belong anywhere, and I knew it, and all my life would be the same, trying to belong, and failing. Always something would go wrong. I am a stranger and I always will be, and after all I didn't really care.

—JEAN RHYS, *Smile Please: An Unfinished Autobiography* (1979)

Contents

Dominica, c.1900

Sargasso Sea

Atlantic Ocean

Capuchin

Hampstead 'Bertrand' Bay

Blenheim

Pointe Baptiste

Cabrits

Hampstead

Calibishie

Portsmouth

Prince Rupert's Bay

Douglas-Charles Airport

Hatton Garden

Morne Diablotin

M A R O O N S

Pagua Valley

CARIB QUARTER

Neg Mawon

Grand Chemin

18th century French dirt track followed by Rhys, 1936

Castle Bruce

Proposed new road

Bells

Layou

Warner

Imperial Road

Caribbean Sea

18th century dirt track Roseau to Rosalie

Rosalie

Massacre

Amelia

Bona Vista

Laudat

Chemin Letang

Canefield

Boiling Lake

Goodwill

Morne Bruce

ROSEAU
(Fort Young)

Pointe Mulatre

Geneva

Stowe

Grand Bay

Soufrière

Scott's Head

Puerto Rico

Virgin Islands

Anguilla

Atlantic Ocean

Barbuda

St Kitts & Nevis

Antigua

Guadeloupe

Dominica

Martinique

Caribbean Sea

St Lucia

St Vincent & Grenadines

Barbados

Grenada

Trinidad

0   2 miles

0   2 km

Foreword

The reason that I always think of Jean Rhys as a hurt and angry child trapped in the body of a sensual woman is that I came to her work, not through her novels or stories, but through *Smile Please*. Written at the end of her long life, in a voice as clear as though she were recalling yesterday's events, Rhys's evocative, tender and painfully truthful memoir describes the first years of her life in Dominica, the wild and still untamed Caribbean island where she grew up—and where she said that she wanted her bones one day to lie. *Smile Please* ends in 1924, five years after Rhys had unregretfully exchanged a hand-to-mouth existence in London for a vagabond's life in Paris, the city which would provide the setting for her first novel, *Quartet*.

Later, as I read the short stories and the five novels on which Rhys's enduring reputation as one of the best women writers of the twentieth century justly stands, I began to understand the tremendous importance of those early years in Dominica. Memories of the island haunt Rhys's work; they inhabited her mind until her death in 1979.

Seeing Dominica with my own eyes while visiting the places that Rhys knew and loved best—all her family's former residences are now destroyed or buried under a verdant island's lush, fast-growing vegetation—helped me to understand Rhys's passion for her Caribbean birthplace, and why the hostility that she first sensed there bred her enduring feeling of alienation. She poured both the passion and the alienation into the characters of the women about whom she wrote. Self-knowledge meant everything to Rhys. Each of those fictional women was granted elements of their author's pitilessly scrutinised personality. As painfully self-aware as their creator, they, too, can be by turns watchful; shocking; angry; witty, and ruthless. Like Rhys herself, they learn to rely on drink for courage and consolation. Unlike her, they neither read much—Rhys was an avid and discerning reader, especially of French poetry and modern French fiction—nor do they write.

"I must write," Rhys once wrote in a private diary, before adding that it was only by her writing that she could "earn" death. ("A reward?" she asked herself in the same entry, and answered, simply: "*Yes*."[1]) Deprived of their author's crucial sense of purpose, the women who belong to the world of Rhys's bleak and often savagely comic fictions are more helpless than their strong-willed—and often downright wilful—maker ever was.

Rhys needed to be strong in order to keep faith with her vocation. I can't think of another woman writer of her time who overcame such dismaying and ongoing setbacks with such determination. Nor can I think of one who created so many problems for herself by her transgressive behaviour: a persistent and audaciously perverse refusal ever to comply with what was expected from her. Heartbreak, poverty, notoriety, breakdowns and even imprisonment: all became grist to Rhys's fiction-making mill. What she never wrote about were the challenging years of literary oblivion from which "Jean Rhys" emerged at last into a blaze of international celebrity that the reclusive writer had neither sought nor desired.

Today, Rhys's work is widely taught. Young graduates who know nothing about her life find it easy to relate to her proud and vulnerable loners. Teachers like to suggest an exercise in which comparisons are made between Virginia Woolf's celebrated "room of one's own" and one of the coffin-like hotel rooms in which Rhys's victimised characters hide away from a world they dread and despise. Students like the concept of Woolf's idealised private study. They *believe* in Rhys's imagined haunts.

Imagined? Rhys did experience times of forlorn desperation when she lived in just such rooms. But not always. In the same way that she bestowed only specific traits from her personality on her characters, she allowed them to experience some—but never all—of her own adventures. Rhys was a novelist, not a journalist. Much was added;

much more was withheld. Researching this book and talking to the people who knew Rhys have helped me to appreciate the depth of the chasm that separates the composite creature whom many critics still knowingly categorise as "the Rhys woman" from the writer who created that vulnerable entity.

Rhys often said that she wrote about herself because that was all she knew. Today, her readers still intuitively relate to a voice that whispers terrible truths into the ears of each and every one of us. I hope that I've succeeded in showing what courage and faith it took to create that unique voice, and to persist when hope seemed dead. I know already how much I shall miss the daily company of a demanding, volatile, self-absorbed and often darkly funny writer, a woman whom the hypercritical Francis Wyndham once fondly praised as the most bewitching companion that he had ever known.

I used to live here once

I

A WORLD APART
Gwen

ELIZÉ MALEWÉ

Tout mama ki ti ni jen fi
Pa lésé yo allé en plési yo,
Pa lésé yo allé en jewté yo.
Si diab la vini yi kai anni mé yo.
Elizé malewé
Elizé malewé
Elizé malewé.
On pon innocen la ou van ba de demon la.

All mothers with young daughters!
Don't let them go follow their own pleasures,
Don't let them go follow their joy.
If the devil comes, he will just take them away.
Poor Elizé
Poor Elizé
Poor Elizé.
You took an innocent child and sold her to the two devils.
(Translation by Sonia Magloire-Akba, with thanks.[*])

[*] The largest single holding of Jean Rhys's personal papers is at the handsomely Gothic-styled McFarlin Library, which forms part of the University of Tulsa, Oklahoma. The library contains a digitalised recording of Jean Rhys singing this old island song in July 1963, when she was almost seventy-three years old. I'm grateful to Sonia Magloire-Akba, an authority on the Kwéyòl (Creole) language still in use today on Dominica, for her informal translation.

1

Wellspring (1890–1907)

"You turn to the left and the sea is at your back, and the road
goes zigzag upwards . . . Everything is green, everywhere
things are growing . . . That's how the road to Constance is—
green, and the smell of green, and then the smell of water and
dark earth and rotting leaves and damp."

—Jean Rhys, *Voyage in the Dark*, Part Three (1934)

NEAR TO THE end of her long life—she was almost ninety when she
died in May 1979—Jean Rhys wrote what her Devonshire neighbour
William Trevor praised as one of the finest short ghost stories he'd
ever read. She called it "I Used to Live Here Once." The dreaming
narrator—evidently Rhys herself—follows the trail of stepping stones
that guide her across a shallow, familiar river and onto a rough forest
path that leads to her own childhood home. She feels "extraordinarily
happy." But when she walks across the parched grass to where a boy and
girl seem to await her, they register her presence and timid greeting
only as a sudden chill in the afternoon air. The children turn away. The
story ends abruptly: "It was then that I knew."

Rhys lived in a secluded village in the south-west of England for the
last nineteen years of an extraordinary and often reckless life, one that
took her from poverty, imprisonment and obscurity to eventual recog-
nition as perhaps the finest English woman novelist of the twentieth
century. The island which haunted her mind and almost everything

that she wrote lay on the far side of the world. There—not in Devon, or London, nor even in Paris—lay the wellspring of Rhys's art.

———————

JEAN RHYS WAS born on 24 August 1890 in Dominica, a small and sternly beautiful Caribbean island of green mountains (*mornes*), tangled forests, rushing rivers, forest pools and impenetrable ravines. Dominica's larger neighbours—Martinique and the archipelago that forms Guadeloupe—were French, as Dominica itself had been until the island was ceded to the British in 1763, at the end of the Seven Years' War. By the close of the nineteenth century, when Dominica had almost 29,000 inhabitants, the island's white population had shrunk to fewer than a hundred. Living in an impoverished outpost of the British Empire, white Dominicans clung to a romanticised vision of England as the centre of their own diminished world, marooned on an island that still spoke in the French-based creole language known today as Kwéyòl.

Jean Rhys's father, William Rees Williams, was a Welshman with an Irish mother. A ship's doctor, he came to Dominica in 1881 in search of better pay as a twenty-seven-year-old British-funded medical officer. He went ashore at the tiny coastal village of Stowe in the area known as Grand Bay, lying below the once prosperous plantation of Geneva in the south-east of the island. In January 1882, the Welshman married Minna Lockhart, a white Creole, a term which, despite its pejorative sound, meant only that Minna, whose family still inhabited Mitcham, the old Geneva estate house, had been born on Dominica. The newlywed couple spent their honeymoon year at Stowe. Dr. Rees Williams brightened the sitting-room walls of their little shoreside home with the four prints of Betws-y-Coed in Snowdonia that had adorned his shipboard cabin. In 1885, Williams was promoted from a relatively humble job in the island's Southern Medical District to a more lucrative position in the capital town of Roseau, where private patient care usefully augmented his income. Here, after renting a house near to the Roseau river on Hillsborough Street (where Jean Rhys was born), the doctor purchased a more substantial property closer to the centre of town.

The Lockhart twins. Rhys's proud mother Minna (*left*) and (*right*) her unmarried, more cultured twin sister, Brenda ("Auntie B") grew up at Geneva, formerly a slave-owning sugar estate, on the Caribbean island of Dominica. (*McFarlin*)

It was burly, hazel-eyed Willie Rees Williams who named the couple's fourth child Ella Gwendoline. Gwen, as she was always known to her relatives, followed two older brothers, Edward and Owen, and a sister named Minna, like their mother. A fifth child, a girl, died as an infant, three years before the birth in 1895 of Brenda Clarice, named both for Minna Lockhart's adored twin (Brenda) and the doctor's devoted sister (Clarice Rees Williams).[*]

Pale-skinned, sapphire-eyed and exceptionally sensitive in spirit,

---

[*] There is dispute about whether it was a slightly older or younger sister who died. Rhys herself had no doubt: "My mother had . . . two sons first, whom she really liked, then a daughter, then me, and after me, a little daughter who died . . . " (Jean Rhys to David Plante, nd, McFarlin, Plante Papers, 1987–007.15.f3). In "Heat," an unashamedly autobiographical story set in 1902 (see Jean Rhys, *The Collected Short Stories*, Penguin, 1987. p. 283), the narrator mentions regular visits to the grave "of my little sister." It seems best to trust Rhys herself on this unresolved issue.

Gwen resembled neither of her parents, nor her more heavily built and dark-haired siblings. Almost from birth, as Rhys remembered it in *Smile Please* (a memoir which still remained unfinished when she died), she had felt like an outsider; a changeling; a ghostly revenant in the hard light of day. True or not, that was the role which would come to fit both the writer and her work as closely as a handstitched glove.

––––––––––––––

NO FAMILY PAPERS survive against which to test the accuracy of *Smile Please*, Jean Rhys's published account of the seventeen years she spent in the West Indies. An unpublished novel by her brother Owen related the story of a white Creole girl who breaks her family's unspoken social code by falling in love with an island boy. But it was Owen—not his sister—who was sent away from Dominica for forming intimate relationships with local girls (one was an employee in his parents' home), an infringement that embarrassed his strait-laced mother. Nothing in Rhys's own recollections suggests that any such romance took place in her early life, although Antoinette Cosway in *Wide Sargasso Sea* recalls having exchanged a final "life and death kiss" with her handsome illegitimate cousin Alexander ("Sandi") before she travels to England as Rochester's wife.[1] Hearsay in the family of Rhys's father's medical colleague Sir Henry Nicholls suggested that Gwen had been labelled "fast" as a young girl. Nicholls and his wife were probably recalling Gwen's childish crush on their son Willie, a youth whose wild ways would eventually lead to his discreet banishment to Scotland, to study medicine.[2]

Travel writers and historians (among them the lushly romantic Lafcadio Hearn and earnest James Froude) have provided magnificent descriptions of Dominica's invincible appearance: a small island rearing up from a range of submerged volcanic peaks like an emerald cathedral of soaring rock. A voracious reader throughout her life, Rhys became familiar with the books written by Froude and Hearn. (Froude toured the island with one of Gwen's Lockhart uncles in the 1880s, as an unofficial representative of Britain's Colonial Office; Hearn, visiting the

West Indies for two years just before Rhys was born, first wrote about Dominica with a lyricism that artfully concealed the fact that he was describing its forested heights from aboard a passenger ship.)

But Jean would remember Dominica best from her own early experiences. She had seen the gigantic wheel and iron mangles at Geneva's disused sugar mill (one of sixty mills on the island from which a cluster of white planters had once prospered); she had listened to the family stories told about her own mother's Lockhart forebears, once the wealthiest of a small plantocracy. The island held a more powerful grasp on her imagination through the enduring presence in her mind of an unforgettable landscape: the green and densely mantled mountains that Rhys knew from childhood as Morne Micotrin, Morne Anglais, Morne Trois Pitons and—towering above them all—Morne Diablotin. They offered a majestic presence, along with a rich stew of gossip, island stories and family scandals that would nourish Jean Rhys's fiction.

Questions abound. How much of the material on which Rhys seems to draw for her novels was based on historical fact? Should a reader believe in the actual existence of Maillotte Boyd, simply because Anna Morgan, the dream-laden protagonist of Rhys's third novel (*Voyage in the Dark*), remembers having seen Maillotte's name on an old list of house-slaves? Does a real Maillotte gain credibility because Rhys also made use of her unusual name in *Wide Sargasso Sea*? (There, in Rhys's extraordinary prequel to *Jane Eyre*, Maillotte's daughter appears both as the twin spirit and the nemesis of unhappy Antoinette Cosway, Mr. Rochester's young Creole wife.) More likely, Rhys was playing with a name that chimes with the word "*mulatto*," a term still in use on Dominica today. Mixed race was not uncommon in families like hers. James Potter Lockhart, Minna's grandfather, had taken two of his slaves as mistresses. Gwen, from an early age, was discouraged from making friends with any of the darker-skinned Lockhart cousins on the island, cousins whose fortunes began slowly ascending as those of her poorer white relatives fell.

RHYS'S FIRST MEMORIES were of the freehold house in Dominica's capital, Roseau, that her father, a proud Welshman, named Bod Gwilym ("William's Home"). A large timber-framed corner house, standing between Cork Street and Grandby Street, Bod Gwilym was painted white, with green-shuttered windows. Gwen's bedroom gave onto a high platform, hidden from public view. From here, as a secret observer, she watched the village women striding down to the marketplace near the bay, dark heads crowned by their bright baskets of mangoes, yellow passionfruit and small, green oranges. Dominica was a Catholic island: there was uproar when an outspoken newspaper editor—described in Rhys's early story "Against the Antilles" as "a stout little man of a beautiful shade of coffee colour" who lived close to the Rees Williams's house—criticised the money being spent on a new palace for the town's Catholic bishop. When a band of angry women marched into town ("Against the Antilles" described the crowd as "throwing stones and howling for the editor's blood"), the shutters of Bod Gwilym were closed and barred. Peeping over the edge of her hidden observation platform, Gwen saw the exhilaration in the women's faces and understood it. As with the mob on the street, so it was indoors between Minna Lockhart and her timid, fiery daughter. Rage might hurt others; never oneself. Rage brought relief.

Standing with her family at an open window and dressed in her best clothes, little Gwen watched the town's annual carnival with longing, waiting for the moment when she was allowed outside, just long enough to present a sixpence to the tall stilt-walker who always stopped to perform a stiff-legged dance beside Dr. Rees Williams's house. Passionately, Gwen had wanted to join the whirling dancers, but she distrusted the brightly daubed wire masks that screened their watchful eyes from view. Once, not perhaps intending to frighten a nervous child, a kitchen visitor spoke in a strange falsetto voice and thrust a thick pink tongue through the white wire mesh that concealed darker skin. Gwen ran away crying. She was inconsolable. Later, Rhys would place that scene among Anna Morgan's Caribbean recollections in *Voyage in the Dark*.

Grandest of all Roseau's public spectacles were the religious processions led by the Catholic bishop and a retinue of stately priests in splendid robes. Watching from the broad wooden gallery that separated the doctor's house from the street, young Gwen gazed out at a dazzle of colourful headdresses, banners and effigies. Listen hard enough, and she could hear the froufrou crackle of paper-hemmed petticoats worn under the ladies' sweeping trains.

Catholicism played no active part in Gwen's home life, but her father, the product of an Anglican upbringing in South Wales, often lunched with a friendly priest and he offered free medical advice at the Catholic Presbytery and the town's convent school. Dr. Rees Williams was not considered a prejudiced man. He saw his white patients privately in the afternoons, but his mornings at the surgery which formed an extension wing to his house were reserved for the black islanders. All patients, black or white, were treated with equal courtesy and only Minna Lockhart raised objections when the doctor despatched his socially sensitive daughter to walk along the surgery queue with small offerings of bread or money.

The doctor's wife cared more than her husband for how she, a proud Lockhart (one sister had married John Spencer Churchill, a former Governor of the Virgin Islands), would be perceived by those whom she regarded as her peers. Gwen's father seems to have quietly favoured Catholicism although he was never a churchgoer, but on Sunday mornings, Minna Rees Williams and her children processed slowly up the hill from Bod Gwilym to St. George's, the town's Anglican church, built for the benefit of the island's leading white families. A pause was always made beside the tiny grave of Gwen's dead baby sister before the doctor's wife swept on to take her position in a pew near the head of the nave, the preserve of the town's white worshippers. Sometimes, bored of watching her mother fan her broad, expressionless face with a fronded palm leaf, Gwen tried to translate an impressive Latin wall tablet that honoured her great-grandfather, James Potter Lockhart. She learned a few of the punning words by heart, well enough to make later use of them, over and again, in her work: *Locked Hearts I open. I have the heavy key.*[3]

Rhys could always summon up Bod Gwilym in vivid detail. A framed dark print of Mary Queen of Scots being led to her execution hinted at the doctor's Catholic sympathies. Recent copies of *The Lancet* and *Cornhill* magazine lay beside the armchair in which he relaxed on the long wooden gallery facing towards the street. Ripe mangoes dropped from the glossy-leaved garden tree that shaded both the smoky kitchen quarters and the cool, windowless room in which a vast stone trough of dark green water served as the family's bath. Gwen preferred to wade—she disliked swimming—deep into one of the island's innumerable forest pools.

The exactness and ease with which Jean Rhys could always evoke her family's home in Roseau suggests that the town was where she had spent most of her early life. The memories were not always happy ones. Evening expeditions with her sea-loving father, rowing her across a wide bay spangled with tiny lights from the Roseau fishing boats, filled a nervous child with a dread that she failed to conceal. "You're not my daughter if you're afraid of being seasick," a father chides the narrator of one of Rhys's most troubling stories, "The Sound of the River." "You're not my daughter if you're afraid of the shape of a hill, or the moon when it is growing old. In fact you're not my daughter."[4]

Less frightening was the annual summer journey in the hollowed-out trunk of a tree up the island's west coast to Massacre. Gwen wouldn't register until later that the village's grim name recorded the murder in 1674 of Carib Warner, stately Sir Thomas Warner's half-white rebel son, or that the English troops confronting him were led by the renegade's white half-brother. For Gwen, Massacre simply marked the place where the Rees Williams family disembarked with their provisions, ready for the slow horseback ride up the 200-foot ascent to her personal favourite of their two summer homes.

Bona Vista was impetuously purchased by the doctor shortly after his move to Roseau, together with a smaller and almost adjoining inland estate called Amelia. Bona Vista stood high above the sea. Writing *Voyage in the Dark* in the early Thirties, Rhys gave them a combined identity with a Welsh name: "Morgan's Rest." From Bona Vista, she remembered: a hammock; a spyglass with which to spot the yellow flags of anchored, quarantined ships; a shadowy drawing room in which the children played halma and bezique on stormy afternoons; her father cradling a nervous, weeping wife in his arms while a high wind rattled the shutters and thunder rolled across the mountains. Evoking an unnamed Bona Vista in the early story she would title "Mixing Cocktails," Rhys dwelt less upon her family's "very new and very ugly house," a bungalow on stilts, than on slow, dreamy days of watching the distant sea change from "a tender blue, like the dress of the Virgin Mary," to a glitter of midday light and, finally, a rich sunset purple that she thought unique to the Caribbean ("The deepest, the loveliest in the world . . . ").*

Bona Vista was where Rhys would choose to open the late memoir she named *Smile Please*. Posed centre stage for a photograph recording a family play—it had been arranged to honour her sixth birthday—Gwen wore a new white dress and a scented wreath of frangipani flowers. So attired, an improbable Red Riding Hood sat perched between her parents, all ready to receive a well-staged visit from her brothers; but Edward, the eldest boy, refused to perform in his role as the honest woodcutter, and Owen's listless growls as he represented the wolf (in a trailing white sheet), failed to convince. Happy endings have no place in Rhys's work. She remembered only a little girl's sadness as she stared down at a picture of Miss Muffet and a hungry spider in the storybook (a birthday gift from Gwen's grandmother in faraway South Wales) hesitantly placed on her lap as a consolation.

Gwen liked her older sister, Minna. She would miss the twelve-year-old girl when she went to live on another Caribbean island with the childless John Spencer Churchill and his wife, Edith (Gwen's little-known "Aunt Mackie"), as the couple's unofficially adopted daughter.

---

* "Mixing Cocktails" and "Against the Antilles" were published in *The Left Bank: Sketches and Studies of Present-Day Bohemian Paris* by Jonathan Cape in 1927. Like *Voyage in the Dark* (Constable, 1934), these stories reflect Rhys's earliest memories of the island more precisely than her later work.

Dominica has more than 300 rivers. Rhys loved bathing in the island's forest pools, some of which are fed by waterfalls. *(Author picture)*

Little Brenda was too young to become a playmate. Left in the company of her older brothers, Gwen felt excluded: a hanger-on. At the smaller Amelia estate (retained after the improvident doctor sold Bona Vista in order to save money), their tumbledown summer home was enclosed by broad mountains and luxuriant woods. Sometimes, Gwen trailed Edward and Owen when they set off armed with an old gun, exploring trails that led deep into the tangled green jungle. Once, wandering off on a separate track, away from the crackle of gunfire, she found herself standing alone and trembling with fear in an open, sunlit glade. *Was* she alone? "The sunlight was still, desolate and arid. And you knew something large was behind you. But what? A stranger? A ghost? You ran," Rhys would later write about Julia Martin's memory of a similar childhood adventure in her second novel, *After Leaving Mr Mackenzie*. "But when you got home you cried."[5]

Gwen saw little of her hard-working father at Bona Vista, since the ride up from his Roseau surgery took over three hours. At Amelia, however, where he tried to make a little money from growing crops, the doctor paid longer visits. Sometimes, he took his daughter along with him to examine a row of young nutmeg trees: in *Voyage*, Anna Morgan's alert pair of eyes are sharp enough to help her father spot the critical difference between a male and female bud.

In Rhys's memories, her father had always been gently encouraging, unjudgemental, trying to do what was best for his favourite child, while her mother missed no opportunity to crush and humiliate a daughter of whom she was perhaps a little jealous. She remembered how Minna Lockhart put an end to Gwen's zealous attempts to teach the Amelia estate's illiterate overseer to read, warning her that John's jealous, cutlass-carrying wife might not appreciate the favour. When one of John's village friends offered Mrs. Lockhart the princely dowry of one large yam to purchase her pretty daughter as his child bride, Minna shared the news with Gwen's siblings and led the chorus of mockery. (And what would such a bride be required to do, young Gwen wondered after being puzzled and upset by the sight of her pet fox-terrier, Rex, rutting in a public place? Her mother wouldn't say. Sex was a forbidden topic.)

Gwen was only three or four when she was taken on her first visit to Geneva, connected to Roseau by a steep and treacherous bridle track that ran south and then east across the southern end of the island before winding uphill to Mitcham House, the original family home of the Lockharts. Later, in one of the coloured exercise books which recorded her private thoughts and episodes for use in her fiction, Rhys wrote that Geneva—thinly disguised as "Constance" in *Voyage in the Dark*—was where she turned four. She remembered the exact year and setting because it was on her fourth birthday, in August 1894, that a local woman, young Elisa Farsa, shot herself on the public road, where a shoreside, slave-descended community were housed below the bluff that protected the Lockharts' home from attack. Within the privacy of her notebooks, Rhys recorded Elisa's name, the date and the place of her death over and again, sometimes changing her name to "Elisa Blank," but without ever offering any explanation.[6] Why did Elisa Farsa's name carry such significance for Gwen? How had the poor young woman obtained a gun? Always discreet about a brother, Owen, who fathered two families on the island, and about her own father, a man who evidently enjoyed the company of women other than his wife, the older Rhys was never prepared to say. All she would acknowledge in *Smile Please*, a memoir written in her eighties, was that the doctor would "flirt outrageously" with any attractive visitor to their home, and that her mother might have minded more than she ever showed.

Riding from Roseau to Geneva one day with Aunt Brenda, her mother's unmarried twin sister, as her guide, Gwen admired the stoicism with which her aunt continued the difficult, three-hour journey, despite having broken several ribs along the way when she was thrown off by her skittish mare. The Lockhart twins prided themselves on their riding skills. Timid Gwen preferred her father's docile nags, Preston and March, to Aunt Brenda's wild-eyed mount. Years later, Rhys would fondly name Antoinette Cosway's obedient horse "Preston."

Brenda Lockhart had helped to nurse Willie Rees Williams back to health when he fell ill shortly after his arrival on the island back in 1881. But if Aunt Brenda had briefly shared her twin's hopes of exchanging an isolated life at Geneva for marriage and children, she bore no apparent grudge. To Gwen, it seemed that her mother, a silent, wary woman, only smiled and laughed when Brenda was with her, little though the twins appeared to have in common. Minna, despite a fondness for the lurid romances of Marie Corelli, disliked books, hated cleverness in a woman and saw no merit in giving her daughters an education. Brenda enjoyed the novels of Rhoda Broughton, a clever, progressive-minded writer who was regularly invited to dine alone with the ageing, London-based Henry James. Minna ordered two evening dresses a year from a London designer. Aunt Brenda, who dabbled in art, loved the theatre and wore dashing hats and the gowns she herself designed and stitched as skilfully as any French-trained couturier.

At Geneva, the unmarried Brenda Lockhart shared Mitcham House with the Woodcock sisters. Julia Lockhart, Gwen's long-widowed granny, was a chatty old lady from St. Kitts whose favourite companion was the green parrot that perched, squawking, on her shoulder. Gwen's granny would eventually provide Aunt Cora's salty warning to Antoinette Cosway against marrying Mr. Rochester, although Granny

Lockhart's comment ("not if his bottom was stuffed with diamonds") was toned down for the readers of *Wide Sargasso Sea*.[7] Gwen formed a closer relationship with Julia's unmarried sister, Jane Woodcock—a sprightly Victorian figure who once created, just for Gwen, an exquisite cardboard doll's house: "Cardboard dolls with painted faces, cardboard tables and chairs, little tin plates for the dolls' meals."[8] The house and its tiny inhabitants were Miss Woodcock's consolation gift after a weeping Gwen confessed to having smashed a coveted doll that had been bestowed upon her little sister.

Gwen first heard the family history of the Lockharts from Jane Woodcock. The old lady didn't always get the details right, but the version she provided took firm root in the mind of an impressionable child. Describing the fiery end of a decaying plantation house in *Wide Sargasso Sea*, Rhys modelled her account on Miss Woodcock's descriptions of a marooned and besieged Geneva.

Long ago—as Aunt Jane explained—back in the 1760s, a family of French Protestants called Bertrand had given Geneva its name when they settled there during the island's French occupation. (Calvinist Geneva had previously provided the Bertrands with a Swiss haven in Europe during times of religious persecution.) Sixty years later, Gwen's acquisitive Lockhart forebear added Geneva to his growing portfolio of Dominican estates. James Potter Lockhart became rich; the dispossessed Bertrands vanished from history. Rhys was still brooding on the Lockharts' takeover of Geneva when she gave the Bertrand family's name to the most heartlessly treated figure in her last and best-known novel. "Who would have thought that any boy could cry like that?" demands an uncomprehending Mr. Rochester when the gentle island-bred Bertrand, known to him only as "the nameless boy," weeps at being abandoned by the man he so admires: "For nothing. Nothing. . . ."[9]

Gwen hated everything Jane Woodcock told her about James Lockhart. Twice Governor of Dominica, the Scottish-born and London-bred businessman had made his fortune from the sugar mills that could crush a weary arm to pulp, and by the profitable trafficking of slaves

When Rhys was a child, she loved to visit her unmarried great-aunt Jane Woodcock (*right*), who lived at Mitcham House, Geneva with her sister, Rhys's grandmother. The third figure (*left*) is unidentified but may be Brenda Lockhart, Rhys's aunt. *(Hesketh Bell papers, Royal Commonwealth Society, Cambridge)*

from one island estate to another. Oil portraits of the white-haired planter and his pretty wife were prominently displayed in the dining room at Mitcham House; well out of view (and unportrayed) were the planter's two slave-mistresses and their dark-skinned descendants: Gwen's Lockhart cousins.

Jane Woodcock talked bluntly about an unscrupulous planter she had never known, whose fortune was made by driving harsh bargains during the last years in which slavery in the West Indies was still legal. Understandably, she spoke with more affection about James Lockhart's son Edward, the man who had married her sister Julia. Perhaps Jane had never been told the truth about what happened six years before Julia and she came to Mitcham House from St. Kitts in 1850. Gwen learned from her only that Edward Lockhart had valiantly rebuilt the house she knew after its precursor had been burned to the ground by a rebel workforce. She heard that her grandfather Edward was "a mild man" and a kind employer. None of these statements was true.

In June 1844, a British attempt to gather statistics for an island census had aroused understandable fears of some cunning new form of enslavement among Dominica's former slave population. When hints of a minor rebellion began to surface, suspected insurgents were brutally suppressed. One man was hanged for throwing a stone which had grazed the cheek of an estate owner. At Geneva, two women protesters were personally flogged by the sugar-mill manager, while "mild" Edward Lockhart joined forces with a local schoolteacher to vandalise the wooden fieldside homes of his workers. With Lockhart's approval, the severed head of one alleged rebel was displayed on a pike.

Inevitably, there were reprisals. Talking to Gwen, old Jane Woodcock painted a lurid picture of angry workers burning Mitcham House to the ground. But the house that the former slaves destroyed had in fact belonged to the sadistic sugar-mill manager. All that Edward Lockhart lost were some of his chattels (beds, chairs, two pianos), which were carried out of his home and burned within view of Mitcham's shuttered windows.

Dominica's press did not hold back about the barbarous flogging of two women at the Geneva estate in the summer of 1844. In London, a disapproving House of Commons heard reports of "most wanton acts of cruelty" undertaken by "an attorney" at Geneva.[10] (Edward Lockhart was a magistrate with legal powers.) Out on the island of Dominica, sympathy was in short supply for the destruction of Mrs. Lockhart's pianos.

———————————

THERE WERE ALWAYS two worlds in Gwen's life on Dominica and she made no secret of which of the two she preferred. It wasn't in the company of her family that she stood on the shivering edge of the island's treacherous Boiling Lake, where a volcanic underworld bubbled into view. Her mother could understand the Kwéyòl language, but it wasn't Minna Lockhart or Gwen's brothers who taught her the saucy words of local songs, or introduced her to the harrowing tales handed down by the French-speaking slaves of a former French colony to their freed descendants. Rhys may even have been drawing on a personal memory for her account of Antoinette Cosway running away as a child to live "with the fishermen and the sailors on the bayside," before she is brought safely home to Coulibri.[11]

Beyond the careful ritual of life in Dr. Rees Williams's townhouse lay the vivid and forbidden world of the islanders. Describing the outspoken Martinique-born Christophine (who functions as Antoinette Cosway's ally and spokeswoman in *Wide Sargasso Sea*), Rhys drew on personal memories of Anne Truitt, a tall, quiet woman who worked as a cook at Bona Vista—and later, at Mitcham House—until her arrest and conviction for practising obeah. Some form of voodoo was often secretly practised by the workforce of a colonial household in the 1890s; late on in life, Rhys casually remarked that Dominicans used to travel to Haiti to study obeah just as English students went to Oxford and Cambridge.[12]

Obeah was widespread in the West Indies during Gwen's childhood. Gwen could easily have learned about it from "Francine," the island-born girl whom Rhys would later describe as the closest friend of her childhood. Francine, first characterised in *Voyage in the Dark* as a free spirit with an enchanting gift for storytelling, led Gwen into a world that was meant to be hidden from a girl of her own class and colour. The abruptness with which an adolescent Francine disappeared from Gwen's life was noted as sad, but unsurprising. An explanation, so Rhys opaquely commented in *Smile Please*, could be surmised. As with Elisa Farsa, a connection of the illicit kind practised by Gwen's hated great-grandfather with his female slaves seems to be lurking here, just out of view. Was Francine compelled to leave after becoming involved with a male member of Gwen's family? It's far from impossible.

Part of Francine's attraction for Gwen lay in the fact that such inter-racial friendships were frowned upon by a mother who was mocked in the Dominican newspapers for her haughty ways. Minna wanted her daughter to mix only with the well-dressed English children who occasionally visited Roseau with their parents from abroad, or from other islands. The British-born doctor was swift to grasp what his white Creole wife failed to understand: such aspirations were doomed to failure. Just as Gwen had been taught to keep her distance from village children, so visitors from England instructed their daughters to stay away from a mere colonial, a girl with a singsong accent, one who had never been to London and who actually enjoyed bathing naked in a river. The sense of not belonging—one which would become central to Rhys's work—was born in the cruel, caste-conscious little world of Roseau. The only certain refuge lay in the books which Gwen began to read—after a start so slow that her parents grew concerned—as soon as she could spell out the words on a page. From that moment on, there was no holding her back.

2

Floggings, School and Sex
(1896–1906)

> "Will you dance Loobi Loobi Li
> Will you dance Loobi Loobi Li
> Will you dance Loobi Loobi Li
> As you did last night?"
>
> —Old island poem quoted by Jean Rhys, 1975[1]

NO RECORD SURVIVES of the books Gwen read as a child, other than those mentioned in the incomplete memoir she wrote during her eighties. *Smile Please* tells us that, before she went to school and started exploring the town library, Gwen devoured the books kept at her Roseau home in an unlocked glass cabinet. *Treasure Island*; *Robinson Crusoe*; *Gulliver's Travels*; a few volumes of poetry that included Byron and Milton: the brisk little list reveals that Rhys already preferred fiction to fact. The row of informative encyclopaedias on the bottom shelf were left untouched.

Books provided a silent but loving connection between Gwen and her Irish grandmother in Wales. Well-read and strong-willed, Sophia Rees Williams had paid out of her own pocket for her second and favourite son to get the medical education he needed to qualify and to travel abroad. Her clergyman husband cared nothing for Willie or his future; a startled Gwen once caught her habitually cheerful father

Bod Gwilym, the Roseau townhouse in which Rhys spent most of her childhood. Boarded up when she revisited the island in 1936, the house was demolished in 2020. *(Author picture)*

shaking his fist at a faded photograph of the crotchetty old Welsh grandfather she never knew.

Twice a year, Granny Sophia sent books to Dominica for a girl who was reported by a proud William to have inherited her own family's good brains. Right up to the last package sent shortly before she died in 1896—it contained the true story of Richard Brinsley Sheridan's romantic elopement with a beautiful young singer—Sophia always intuited just what was wanted.[2]

Gwen's mother took no interest in her daughter's passion for reading; Gwen's nursemaid, Meta, warned the child that her eyes would fall out if she didn't break the habit. It was from Meta, hard-fisted and always in a rage, that Gwen learned that a cockroach, if it flew into her mouth, would leave a bite that would never heal. The threat seemed more real because Gwen's mother would never enter a room where a cockroach had been glimpsed. A white girl like Gwen faced being taunted by passers-by in the streets of Roseau as a "white cockroach": an outsider; the wrong colour on an island which had a predominantly dark-skinned population.

Meta—given an entire chapter to herself in *Smile Please*—thrived on the manufacture of terror, telling stories of red-eyed women who crept into children's bedrooms at night and sucked their blood. Zombies, so Meta said, could open any door; you'd know nothing until a pair of hairy hands locked around your throat. "Meta had shown me a world of fear and distrust," Rhys wrote in her old age and added, pitifully: "I am still in that world."[3]

As with Meta, so it was with her mother. "How did it happen and why?" Rhys would ask herself years later in a private undated note, "that I gradually grew to love and trust my father. Not her."[4] Sharpest in her memory was the torment of being mocked. Meta, having noticed her charge's childish crush on the son of her father's colleague, enjoyed pretending that Willie Nicholls had just called at the Cork Street house, for the fun of seeing a flustered Gwen fumble with the elaborate hooks and buttons of her best frock before rushing downstairs, only to find an empty room. A letter of shy admiration that Gwen planned to send to one of her parents' male friends was opened by her mother, who expressed mocking astonishment: why on earth would a popular gentleman like Mr. Greig want a letter from such an ugly girl? Gwen's tribute was never sent.[5] The cruel putdown, to a girl too young and insecure to recognise her own uncommon beauty, was deeply felt.

There was worse. Meta, when angry, which was often, shook the child until her teeth chattered. Mrs. Rees Williams went further, flogging her daughter with a whip whenever Gwen did something to annoy her. The cause could be as trivial as taking part in an inappropriate game. ("*Will you dance Looby Looby Li, as you did last night?*" Gwen and her friends sang and acted out in a quiet corner of Roseau's ultra-respectable Botanical Gardens, vaguely sensing that they were doing something forbidden.) Often, Gwen was whipped for no reason at all. Years later, confiding her unhappy memories to a black exercise book still preserved among her papers at Tulsa, Rhys would write that her mother saw "something alien" in her daughter: in fact, "she couldn't bear the sight of me."[6] The whippings were still in full force in 1902, when Gwen was twelve years old. "I've done my best," she was told at this point. "You'll never be like other people."[7] An outsider might deduce that Minna Rees Williams was jealous of Gwen's closeness to a father in whose eyes his clever, ardent daughter could do no wrong.

Gwen would never have had an education if her mother had got her way. The Rees Williams boys (their mother's favourites) were sent away to boarding schools in England, returning home to Dominica only once a year. Gwen, aged nine, was sent on her father's insistence to Roseau's Catholic convent as a day girl. The convent's pupils wouldn't mix with the handful of white girls, among whom Gwen found it hard at first to make a friend; eventually, she teamed up with an exotic trio of fellow outsiders—the three South American sisters seeming scarcely younger than the exquisitely dressed mistress who accompanied their debonair father (and his pair of Cuban bloodhounds) on rare visits to the island from abroad.

Gradually, away from her mother, Gwen grew happier, sufficiently so that it didn't distress her, aged thirteen, to board for six months when her parents visited England during the doctor's official leave. The original convent, which survives as a retreat for priests, was based around a small, square-shaped house that still looks much as it did when Gwen arrived at its sturdy doors in 1899. There, taught by a group of intelligent and worldly nuns whose mother convent was located at Norwood in south London, Gwen studied piano and fell in love for the rest of her life with French poetry. Tucked away within the substantial archive of Jean Rhys's notes and drafts and letters held in the McFarlin Library at Tulsa, Oklahoma are a handful of tiny blue pages on which she wrote out—always in French—extracts from poems by Verlaine, Rimbaud, Baudelaire, Hugo, de Musset.[8] In moments of despair, Gwen would always return to poetry, and to the convent's maxims for comfort and encouragement. "Truth is great and will prevail" remained high among her favourites, but the proclamation that Jean Rhys would adopt as her enduring source of inspiration came from Saint Teresa of Ávila: "At the cost of a thousand sufferings, at the cost of a long death before the fact, I will find that country which is new and ever young. Come with me and you will see."

Gwen, when she first arrived at the Virgo Fidelis Convent, had never yet left Dominica. Aged eleven, she was taken by her Aunt Brenda to the town of Castries on Saint Lucia, where Acton Lockhart, head of the white side of Gwen's maternal family, was getting married. In *Smile Please*, Rhys would invoke the crowing of cocks to suggest the dawning of sexual awareness at Castries, where a daring girl trapeze artist from Havana captured all of her attention on a first delighted visit to a circus. At some point shortly after her return to Roseau, conscious of being watched by an admiring young Willie Nicholls, Gwen slid her body down into the green water that always filled the Rees Williamses' massive bathing trough. For the first time, she experienced the power of her physical beauty.

Aged twelve, Gwen was poised between childhood and adolescence. Some of the final whippings inflicted by her mother may have been a

The author in 2018, outside the original little Virgo Fidelis Roseau convent attended by Rhys. *(Author picture)*

punishment for the habit which now began and which the older Rhys buried in a private note, not intended for publication: "I remember that hot day when I locked the window and started. I remember when it got coarse and when it got too bad to bear and when it started to change . . . At last I would have [liked?*illeg.*] for it to stop. I closed my eyes. It helped me to sleep and I knew of course never to give way to despair. It is a sin."⁹

VISITING MITCHAM HOUSE in April 1902, Gwen was woken from sleep and silently led by her mother to watch a molten cloud bloom and spread above the distant hills of Martinique. The fiery cloud proved a harbinger; on 8 May, a massive volcanic eruption buried Martinique's cultural capital, pretty Saint-Pierre, and its forty thousand inhabitants, in burning ash. A few weeks later, Gwen's father joined a boat that went to inspect the devastation of Saint-Pierre—and to gather souvenirs. Dominica's thirty-eight-year-old French-born governor, Henry Hesketh Joudou Bell, brought back a china Madonna that he found clasped in a dead woman's arms: "a wonderful memento of the terrible catastrophe."¹⁰

Gwen's father returned home to Roseau with two church candlesticks, fused together by the heat and twisted into a single blackened trophy which he hung on a dining-room wall in Bod Gwilym as his own souvenir of the tragedy. To Gwen, the entire episode felt unreal, like something in a dream. Many years later, she would draw upon it for a story she called, simply: "Heat."

Shortly before Hesketh Bell's arrival on the island in 1901 for a happy six-year sojourn as Dominica's administrator, the island became a colony of the British crown.¹¹ Encouraged by Joseph Chamberlain at the Colonial Office and backed by his son Neville, the hardworking Hesketh Bell set himself the challenging task of restoring a white plantocracy. In 1903, Bell arranged for the crown to grant Dominica's indigenous people—then known as "Caribs," and now as the Kalinago—control over an unpromising tranche of hilly coastland on the island's eastern side, facing the Atlantic. At the same time, 100,000 acres of fertile land were put up for offer to British settlers with access via a magnificent new road from Roseau that—after encircling their properties—would return to the island's west coast.

Bell's project replaced an earlier and more benign administrator's plan to restore an old French paved track and from it create a bridle path across the island, for the use of all, not just the new settlers. Recalling tales about this earlier project, Gwen would later persuade herself that the Imperial Road itself had spanned the island, and that she had witnessed its ceremonious opening. The sad truth was that Bell's project for a circular Imperial Road ran out of funding after seventeen misguided miles. Gwen was present to witness the grand opening celebration in 1903, complete with trumpets and speeches and gold-braided epaulettes, of the opening of the Canefield Bridge, marking the point where the new road was to begin, three miles north of Roseau. The rebellious Gwen who yearned to become a free spirit, a girl of the island, was briefly displaced by an ardent young imperialist, waving her parasol and clapping her white-gloved hands on a day that marked her island's link to distant, glorious England as the seat of empire.

Impressed by Mr. Bell's appearance in a plumed hat and splendid uniform, Gwen was too innocent to understand that the handsome and unmarried administrator was homosexual. Aged fourteen in 1904, she gladly accepted an invitation to a Christmas fancy dress ball which Mr. Bell was hosting for an adored young niece whose parents, the Scullys, also lived on the island. Gwen's audacious plan to swagger into the Governor's House wearing the close-fitting blue jacket and scarlet bloomers of a Zouave officer was scotched by her conventionally minded mother. Deft-fingered Aunt Brenda came to the rescue, whipping up a sea-green costume with a tight bodice and a full skirt; the convent's nuns added a rustling hem, which they decorated with paper fish. Clothes would always be talismanic for Rhys; she attributed her triumph to the beauty of her dress when the chivalrous Mr. Bell invited her to partner him for the first waltz. He asked her to dance with him

Henry Hesketh Bell, as he may have looked when a shy Rhys encountered him after attending the Governor's fancy dress ball. *(Hesketh Bell papers, Royal Commonwealth Society, Cambridge)*

again and again. Skimming across the floor, watched by all, Gwen thought she had discovered bliss. Now, "I would always be happy."[12]

Riding out of town a few days later, Hesketh Bell spotted Miss Rees Williams ambling towards him on Preston, her favourite mount. He called out a friendly greeting. Overcome by shyness, she couldn't speak. Following a subsequent afternoon game of croquet at Roseau's carefully exclusive Dominica Club, Gwen's mother took good care to report home that Mr. Bell had used the occasion to poke fun at her daughter's timidity. Gwen never spoke to him again.

Self-consciousness was becoming Gwen's greatest enemy. It had given her real joy to be applauded for a piano recital ("the lights and the people clapping and the palm trees") that may have taken place during the visit to Castries with Aunt Brenda.[13] Back at home, more courage was required in order to volunteer herself as the accompanist when Mr. Greig, one of the men she most revered for his sensitivity and cultured ways, offered to play the violin to a group of friends assembled for a musical evening at the Rees Williams' home. Mr. Greig forged ahead; Gwen, unconscious of the significance of the *da capo* (repeat) sign, lost

her way. Instead of helping her out, an icily impolite Mr. Greig laid
down his instrument; to a mortified teenager, it was made clear that
the fault was all her own. Meeting Mr. Greig by chance years later at a
London restaurant, Rhys persuaded herself that he was still scowling
with remembered rage. A searing awareness of herself and of how people responded to her would become a vital element in Rhys's later work
as a writer; even as a young girl, such extreme self-scrutiny imposed a
heavy burden.

Sexuality often runs just beneath the surface of what Rhys published about her early years. She described her father as a generous
man adored by women; she also wrote of the pleasure he took in shar-
ing small acts of intimacy with his favourite daughter. The doctor often
asked pretty Gwen to light his pipe and mix his evening drink ("I mea-
sure out angostura and gin, feeling important and happy . . . "[14]). Her
father's friends enjoyed it when she performed similar tasks for them.
Sometimes, they beckoned the doctor's slender, large-eyed daughter
to perch on their knees. "Baa baa black sheep," one of the first of the
island's new settlers, Mr. Ramage, rumbled in Gwen's ear. Later, Rhys
would shape for public view the true and strange story of how Mr.
Ramage married an islander, became a hermit and once swam down-
stream to Roseau stark naked, with his clothes in a bundle on his head.
But she chose not to tell the world about another house guest, Mr.
Brown, whose waist-length beard tickled her tender skin and gave her
nightmares in which tall, bearded men chased her down dark passages.

Conspicuous by its absence from the pages of *Smile Please* is a dis-
turbing incident upon which Rhys would base "Good-bye Marcus,
Good-bye Rose," one of her most autobiographical short stories. The
names in the title of a short, often rewritten story about twelve-year-old
Phoebe were among those young Gwen had fancifully selected for the
children of the suitable marriage which was her expected destiny as a
colonial girl. ("But she'd always doubted this would happen to her," says
self-aware Phoebe. "Even if numbers of rich and handsome young men
suddenly appeared, would she be one of the chosen?")[15] Well tutored
in guilt by her Catholic teachers at the convent, Gwen construed her

encounter with the sinister Mr. Howard (Captain Cardew in her published story about Phoebe) as evidence of her own innate wickedness. "He must know," states Phoebe of her "seducer." "He knew. It was so."[16]

Gwen was fourteen years old when the Howards—a handsome oldish man and his seemingly bored young wife—visited from a neighbouring island and made friends with her parents. In her private notes, Rhys recalled how she had first approached their distinguished-looking guest and offered to light his cigar, just as she had been schooled by her father. Invited to show the visitor around Roseau's magnificent Botanical Gardens, Gwen gladly agreed. The fictional Phoebe dresses carefully for the expedition in a white blouse, long white skirt, black stockings and black buttoned boots; clothes-conscious Gwen probably did just the same. In the story's published form, Captain Cardew surreptitiously gropes Phoebe's breasts after learning that she is twelve. An earlier exercise book version had revealed Gwen's actual age at the time of meeting Mr. Howard: "Fourteen he says, fourteen is old enough to have a lover . . . His hand of an old man on my breasts felt cold and dead." On the way home, this evidently practised predator talked calmly to her of casual things. "I hardly spoke."[17]

On subsequent visits to the gardens, Mr. Howard invited Gwen to consider herself his slave, ready to be carried off to a distant island where she would obey his every whim: she would be whipped, bound with ropes of flowers, summoned to wait, naked, upon his fully clothed guests. "It fitted like a hook to an eye," Rhys sardonically commented years later in one of four unpublished exercise books. "After all I'd been whipped a lot." Of Phoebe's strange suitor, she wrote that "Captain Cardew" dwelt on the many different ways of making love. "Violence, even cruelty, was an essential part of it."[18]

Precisely when Rhys first chose to record this act of sexual abuse remains unclear. Elsewhere in her private notes, she wrote that Mr. Howard grew nervous after his wife, realising what was going on, had blamed Gwen, calling her a bad girl. When she next offered to light his cigar, he pushed her away.

Recalling the night before the Howards sailed home, Rhys later remembered lying on her secret bedroom platform under enormous, glowing stars, imagining the moment when she, too, would leave the island. "And when I go what will happen to me? Strange treasures, carpets of the East, and the mountains always saying '*Temps perdi, temps perdi*'."*[19]

ESTABLISHING A CHRONOLOGICAL sequence for Gwen's last two years in the West Indies isn't easy. At the convent, the doctor paid for his brightest child to receive extra tuition in French and in music. At home, Gwen spent long hours lolling on the veranda of the new town library, built when she was eleven—energetic Mr. Hesketh Bell was drawing up plans for an even larger, better-stocked one to be funded by Andrew Carnegie—that overlooked Roseau's fishing harbour and the bay. And what did she read? Rhys says almost nothing in her late-written memoir, but it's reasonable to assume that the library introduced her to some of the stalwarts—Dickens, Thackeray, Walter Scott—which Edwardian colonial ladies and their daughters could read without a blush.

But the Victoria library's collection wasn't entirely conventional. Reminiscing in her old age, Rhys described a youthful penchant for stories about prostitutes. Was it here, in a library that collected books from the ships that paused at Roseau on their way to neighbouring French islands, that she first discovered a lifelong favourite? Pierre Louÿs's *Aphrodite* (1896) told the story, in gorgeously erotic prose, of a sculptor in ancient Alexandria and his passion for Chryses, a beautiful courtesan. If so, she kept quiet. Louÿs's extraordinary novel was never publicly mentioned by Rhys, despite her enduring love of it. Instead, recalling the little library's crowded, dusty shelves, she singled out Filson Young's *The Sands of Pleasure*, a hastily written 1905 bestseller about an Englishman's romance with a Parisian demimondaine.

These were not the kind of books a young lady was expected to read.

---

* *Temps perdi*, in Dominica's French-based language, means time that is not "lost," but wasted.

Locked away in her room, dreaming of Parisian trysts, Gwen created more respectable dramas for home performance. Docile, sturdy little Brenda was usually cast as the speechless princess, while the young playwright played the swashbuckling villain.

Every good villain needs an accomplice; perhaps Gwen found a walk-on role for her beloved terrier in the (lost) scripts that she churned out. Heartbroken when Rex suddenly died from distemper, she was consoled with the present of a dress allowance from a doting father who indulged her passion for clothes. Minna Rees Williams, fretting ceaselessly about her husband's extravagance, disapproved; Rhys remembered an occasion on which her mother—while visiting a sympathetic island neighbour—broke down in tears over the family's shrinking resources. The doctor, although he grieved at having to sell Bona Vista, remained blithe and gay; Gwen herself worried more about the poverty that so evidently surrounded them everywhere in Dominica. Later, laughingly, she referred to a conscience-stricken early phase in life when the family nicknamed her "Socialist Gwen." Beyond attempting to teach their overseer to read, no evidence suggests that any of her planned social reforms were ever put into action. Rhys did, however, state in *Smile Please* that she had never been so happy as when, inspired by the sermons in the Anglican church and defended by a loving father from her mother's impatient protestations, she went through a period of doing good deeds.

WHITE CREOLE GIRLS from the Caribbean were traditionally sent to England in order to lose their lilting accents and thus become more eligible for marriage. Brenda, Gwen's younger sister, would eventually attend—war interrupted her progress—a respectably mediocre school in Bloomsbury. Several years earlier, in 1906, word reached Dominica from the doctor's widowed aunt, Jeanette Potts, that clever Gwen, unseen and untested, had been granted a place for the following year at Cambridge's distinguished and academically demanding Perse High School for Girls. In 1906, only one English girl in five was receiving a formal education. Here was a triumph: Clarice Rees Williams, visiting her brother's home from St. Asaph in South Wales early in 1907, volunteered to act as Gwen's chaperone to England.

Rhys would always retain vivid memories of her aunt's six-month stay on Dominica, and of the silent war that was continually being waged between Clarice and her sister-in-law over the doctor's affections. "Poor Willie," Clarice would sigh, hinting that a homesick brother had been kept abroad against his will. Mrs. Rees Williams struck back by retreating to her bed with an unidentified illness that kept her out of view, leaving the busy doctor to arrange picnics, excursions and even a farewell summer dance at the family's home in Roseau, all in honour of his adored—and adoring—daughter.

Minna, distracted by the unpleasing news that Owen, her second and favourite son, had recently fathered a child by an "island girl," had no time for farewells to Gwen. Her husband made up for her wounding indifference. After travelling with his sister and Gwen to Bridgetown in Barbados, the doctor escorted them onto the steamer and seized hold of his daughter in such a tight embrace that he crushed to pieces the little coral brooch that had been his last gift to her. "I had been very fond of it," Rhys later wrote with the calmness of hindsight: "now I took it off and put it away without any particular feeling. Already all my childhood, the West Indies, my father and mother had been left behind. I was forgetting them. They were the past."[20]

A concert was held on board to while away a tedious voyage. Boldly, Gwen volunteered to sing. A pretty voice compensated for a very un-English island lilt: the applause was loud. Elated, and perhaps encouraged by the glamorous accounts of theatre life that her Aunt Brenda had brought back from a recent visit to England, Gwen announced that she intended to go "straight on to the stage" as soon as they reached London.[20] Clarice laughed outright at such an absurd proposal: did her niece honestly imagine that the sober Perse School would tolerate such nonsense? What would her parents say?

Gwen was entirely serious. She felt no wish to return to Dominica or to continue her education. What she wanted was to become a great actress: Britain's very own Sarah Bernhardt. Aged just seventeen in August 1907, Gwen suffered from crippling self-consciousness and fits of anger and despair that she did not know how to control. The compensation came in the moments when, however briefly, she could believe in a glorious future.

II

ENGLAND:
A COLD COUNTRY
*Ella**

"Then, quite suddenly, it seemed, it began to grow cold."

—Jean Rhys, "First Steps," *Smile Please*

---

* A year after arriving in England in 1907, Gwen began to use her first given name: Ella. This was how Rhys would choose to be addressed in her private life during the next fifty years. Shortly after the publication of *Wide Sargasso Sea* in 1966, however, Rhys instructed her own daughter and grandchild to start calling her Jean, "because that is who I am" (Dr. Ellen Moerman to author, 23 January 2019).

3

Stage-struck (1907–13)

"I often wonder who I am and where is my country, and where do I belong . . ."

—Antoinette Cosway, *Wide Sargasso Sea*[1]

DREAMING IN A rocking chair on the broad veranda of the Victoria Memorial Library, set high above Roseau's glittering bay, Gwen Rees Williams had created an idealised Motherland from the books that she devoured. Snow—unimaginable in Dominica—would carpet the fields and "wolds" (whatever they might be). Fires would blaze in every grate. Bright trains, coloured like nursery toys, steamed into a theatre-filled London, a city where handsome gentlemen in gleaming top hats swept deep bows to beautiful ladies with rosy cheeks. A small but sturdy pink England presided over a reassuringly pink map of the world hanging on one of the library walls.

In the summer of 1907, a young colonial girl could confidently picture herself standing at the heart of the glorious Empire. For Rhys, the memory of that enchanting image would never fade. Writing about Antoinette Cosway, half a century later, she would confer on the Caribbean-born heroine of *Wide Sargasso Sea* (1966) precisely the same fantasies of "wolds" and a "rosy pink" Motherland that she would weave into her fragmented autobiography, *Smile Please* (1979).[2]

Arriving at the port of Southampton, Gwen peered out of her cabin's porthole and realised that her imaginary England was no more than a fairy tale: "looking at the dirty grey water, I knew for an instant all that would happen to me. . . ."[3] The train taking her up to London was brown and drab, as was—on an arid afternoon in late August—the great dusty city itself. The next day, disheartened by an early morning stroll around smoke-grimed Bloomsbury, Gwen decided to take a bath at the boarding house where she and Aunt Clarice were staying. Bathing reminded her of home and the pleasure of languid afternoons spent lazing with Francine in Dominica's shadow-spattered forest pools. But a real bath, with taps that ran hot water: this was a novelty. Immersed, she decided to keep the stream of warm water running in. Content at last, Gwen started to sing.

As an older, self-searching writer, Rhys would cite that act of innocent self-indulgence to illustrate how, right from the start, she was made to feel like an outsider in England. The landlady was furious, as was her mortified aunt. Baths were still a luxury in 1907, even among the rich; it's surprising that the boarding house even possessed one to offer to its lodgers. By using up an entire day's supply of hot water, and without seeking permission, Gwen had committed her first offence. How could she be so thoughtless! "I've already noticed," her aunt remarked tartly, "that you are quite incapable of thinking about anyone else but yourself."[4]

Later in life, Rhys would come to appreciate that Clarice Rees Williams had been a thoughtful chaperone to her limp and unresponsive niece. Conducted around the sights of London—Westminster Abbey, St. Paul's, the Wallace Collection, the Zoo—Gwen was unimpressed. How could a girl who grew up on an island alive with exquisite hummingbirds relish seeing those tiny symbols of freedom fluttering in a dark cage with a filthy floor? "The humming-birds," Rhys wrote in *Smile Please*, "finished me."

Gwen's introduction to London was brief. In September, she went as a boarder to the Perse. The school, established in a substantial Georgian villa that stood on Union Road in the heart of Cambridge, had been successfully run for over twenty years by a formidable principal. Katherine Street—always addressed by the pupils as "Madam"—was a handsome woman with an understanding expression and long, thickly waving grey hair which she plaited up into a bun worn like a crown. Fictionalising the school in later years, Rhys unsubtly changed Miss Street's name to Rode. "Miss Born" provided an equally thin disguise for Hannah Osborn, a sharp-faced retired teacher who would eventually share Miss Street's Cambridge grave as her "beloved friend."

Blanche Paterson ("Patey"), the relatively young teacher of classics, was Gwen's favourite among the Perse staff. Patey once took her to

The staff at Perse School in Cambridge, where Rhys attended through the academic year of 1907–8. The principal, Katherine Street, sits centre front with her lifelong companion, Miss Hannah Osborn, seated on her left. *(Used with permission of the Stephen Perse Foundation)*

visit Ely Cathedral, where Gwen was overwhelmed by the grandeur of the stone arches that soared above her. Perhaps their majestic height reminded a homesick girl of Dominica's tall forests; seated at a ceremonious tea intended by Miss Paterson as a treat to complete the day's excursion, Gwen grew so emotional that she dropped her delicate china cup and smashed it.

The teachers were kind, but Gwen's schoolmates proved either tactless or cruelly snobbish. Mocking her singsong Caribbean lilt, they nicknamed the outsider "West Indies"; when *Jane Eyre* was announced as a set book, much fun was had about the fact that Bertha Antoinette Mason, presented by Charlotte Brontë as a red-eyed, grovelling maniac, was a white Creole—just like Gwen. It didn't help that a fire broke out at the school, from a carelessly raked hearth, while the pupils were reading about Bertha Mason's immolation of her husband's Yorkshire manor house. Snide comments were made. The insult to a sensitive spirit was never forgotten or forgiven.

———————

CAMBRIDGE ITSELF LEFT little impression on the newcomer, other than a faint enthusiasm for the Bridge of Sighs and a tender memory of the unknown young man who carefully helped pretty Gwen to her feet when she fell off her borrowed bicycle. On Saturdays, when she cycled out to visit her stately great-aunt's home on Trumpington Road, Gwen was gently teased about her passion for poetry. White-haired and black-eyed, the long-widowed and still captivating Jeanette Potts—sister to Sophia Rees Williams—still retained signs of having been a celebrated beauty. She told Gwen a strange story of once having planned to leave her dour husband, a celebrated Cambridge mathematician, for a lover until she glimpsed the devil in a mirror, leering over her shoulder. Mrs. Potts unpacked her bag and stayed at home.

Gwen liked and respected Mrs. Potts, to whom she most likely owed her introduction to the Perse. Later, writing fragments of recollection in her notebooks, Jean Rhys would conflate this imposing representative of Cambridge's academic world with her beloved great-aunt, out at Geneva. Jane Woodcock had been her loyal ally and favourite story-teller—and yet Gwen never again made contact with her, nor answered the old lady's fond, enquiring letters. Ill at ease though Gwen might have felt in England, she had consciously severed herself from her past.

Mrs. Potts, well connected in the academic world, held out high hopes for her great-niece. The Perse specialised in turning out fine teachers; with diligence, Gwen Williams might even rise to become a headmistress. There was no doubting Gwen's intelligence—she easily won the school's top prize for ancient history—but she was too much of a rebel to embrace a future in the academic world. Dismay was caused when she submitted an essay on *The Garden of Allah*, by Robert Smythe Hichens, for her exam in English literature. The novel, a turgid but surprisingly popular account of a thirty-year-old woman who seeks spiritual meaning during a long journey across the Sahara, was not one of which the Perse approved. Perhaps Gwen picked it on purpose to annoy. By the summer of 1908, she already knew what she wanted to become, and it was not a teacher.

Aged almost eighteen, Gwen remained determined to go on stage. She took confidence from the resounding applause for her perfor-mance, in front of the assembled Perse parents, as the playfully dis-honest Autolycus in *The Winter's Tale*. Playing a male role once again, she was praised for her lively impersonation of the honest provincial, Tony Lumpkin, in Oliver Goldsmith's *She Stoops to Conquer*.

"Overture and Beginners Please," a late Rhys story that began life as an autobiographical vignette, describes the startled pleasure that Gwen felt when a Perse housemaid complimented her performance in the Shakespeare play. But it was one of the mothers—if Rhys's fictional version can be trusted—who provided the necessary spur to action, asking her own daughter to tell the girl who had played Autolycus that she was "a born actress." And then: "She says that you ought to go on the stage and why don't you?"[5] Gwen had already taken that decision when she wrote home to Roseau and asked permission to audition for acting school.

While Aunt Clarice disapproved of Gwen's project as strongly as

did Mrs. Potts, Dr. Rees Williams was pleased that Gwen had chosen
a career for which she seemed to exhibit a genuine talent. Permission
having been granted, the doctor's confidence was rewarded by the news
that his talented daughter had won a coveted place at Sir Herbert Tree's
new Acting School on Gower Street, the first of its kind in England.
Today, we know that same school—greatly enlarged and modernised—
as RADA.

———————

A CAREER ON the English stage in 1909 offered enticing prospects to
an ambitious young woman. The theatre certainly had its disreputable
side, but no stigma attached to becoming a great actress—Ellen Terry,
for example, or Mrs. Patrick Campbell—and Gwen was determined
to become not merely good, but great. Aunt Clarice, while keeping a
close eye on proceedings from a small flat that she had rented on Baker
Street, soon found herself redundant. Gwen, having taken Bloomsbury
lodgings of her own, was working hard. The school was coaching her
in all the skills required for a stage career: gesture, fencing, and ballet.
Elocution was taught by a gentle Mr. Heath until a snobbish senior student overruled his insistent mispronunciation of the word "froth" ("I'm
not here to learn cockney," she shrilled, or so Rhys recalled, decades
later)—and got him sacked.[6]

To Clarice, Gwen reported that her prospects looked good; still
only in her second term, she was regularly playing the lead in rehearsal
scenes chosen from Shakespeare and Oscar Wilde. She wasn't short of
admirers. When a wealthy fellow student called Harry Bewes asked her
to marry him, Gwen told her disconcerted aunt that she had turned the
young man down in order to pursue her vocation.

Gwen's acting apprenticeship was brief. Money was increasingly
scarce in the Rees Williams household and the Tree school charged
high fees. In June 1909, the doctor asked the academy's head, Kenneth
Barnes, for a candid view of his daughter's prospects. Gwen was pay-
ing a dutiful visit to the family of her father's older brother, Neville,
up in Yorkshire when the bad news arrived. Equipped as she was with

a seemingly ineradicable island lilt, Mr. Barnes had advised her father that Gwen could never achieve success as a serious actress. To continue with her lessons was—in Barnes's opinion—a waste of money. Writing to his daughter, Willie Rees Williams gently explained that the time had come to renounce her dreams and return to her home in Roseau.

At the time, Gwen was devastated. Later, Jean Rhys's chief concern would be to conceal the truth. Her father died the following year. By shifting the date of his death back to the previous summer—as she would do both in the story "Overture and Beginners Please" and in her memoir—Rhys managed to blame her swift departure from the acting school on Minna, the doctor's unsympathetic and financially straitened widow. She never mentioned the verdict of Mr. Barnes. But from this time on, she would train herself to speak in a soft, whispering voice that concealed her origins. That cultivated whisper made it all the more shocking on the occasions when a seemingly ladylike young woman lost control over it and vented her fury in a voice that ranted and raved like a daemonic alter ego.

While disguising the reason for her sudden departure, Rhys was honest about the anguish that leaving the Tree school caused her. Fleeing Uncle Neville's Harrogate home to take refuge at her aunt's cosier Welsh cottage, Gwen dissolved into sobs. "You cry without reticence," Aunt Clare remarks in "Overture and Beginners Please." By the time Miss Rees Williams and her downcast niece returned to London from the tiny cathedral city of St. Asaph—Clarice still lived touchingly close to the rectory where she and her brothers grew up at Bodelwyddan—Gwen's mind was already made up: whatever might become of her, she was not going back to Dominica.

Smile Please implies that Gwen's next step was taken on a last-minute impulse, but it's clear that she had formed a plan. While Clarice went shopping, her niece hurried off to London's best-known theatrical agency, Blackmore's, and requested an immediate audition. The approach, born of desperation, was audacious, but Gwen was exceptionally pretty and ready to display a fetching pair of slender ankles while forming the requested few dance steps.

Gwen left Blackmore's armed with a renewable contract and a freshly minted stage name: Ella Gray. She was given orders immediately to join rehearsals with Sir George Dance's second touring company. Her visit had been fortunately timed; the agents were giving the newcomer a chance to join the first summer tour of a musical comedy, *Our Miss Gibbs*, in which "Miss Gray" would form part of a chorus of implausibly glamorous shop assistants at "Garrods." A wage of thirty-five shillings a week was expected to cover her travel, food and lodgings. The gorgeous costumes (sweat-stained hand-me-downs from the dancers in the grander London production of the same show) would be provided free of charge.

Rallying to this abrupt change of direction, Clarice chaperoned her unnervingly determined niece to the designated rehearsal space, a dingy room at the back of a sporting club off Leicester Square. The other girls liked sturdy, old-fashioned Clarice; they weren't so sure about the pale, foreign-sounding girl she had brought along to join them. A friendly gentleman at Blackmore's had already warned Gwen to keep quiet about her aspiration to become a serious actress. Doubtless, he also advised her to set aside any fantasies about marrying a peer. An English lord might—and often did—propose to one of the celebrated Gaiety Girls who frolicked through the London musicals presided over by Mr. George Edwardes (the great impresario of the day). No aristocrat would offer his name to a girl he'd found dancing in the chorus of a mere touring production.

The agent could warn Gwen, but she'd read too many romantic stories for him to crush a young girl's hopes. Together with a small print of herself as a smiling young dancer (one who could also carry a tune), Rhys would lovingly preserve a photograph of pretty Nancy Erwin, a shrewdly knowing London chorus girl with a trademark quip. "My little bit of Scotch," Nancy liked to trill as she flourished a tiny plaid handkerchief. Nancy's marriage turned her into Lady Dalrymple Champneys, while pretty Rosie Boote became the Marchioness of Headfort. Constance Collier, once a Gaiety Girl, married two grandees